Social Media Surveillance and Experiences of Authoritarianism

Göran Bolin, Veronika Kalmus, Rita Figueiras,
& Erik Björklund

Södertörns högskola

Södertörn University
Library
SE-141 89 Huddinge
www.sh.se/publications

Cover layout: Jonathan Robson
Graphic form: Per Lindblom & Jonathan Robson

Stockholm 2023

Mediestudier vid Södertörns högskola 2023:2
ISSN 1650-6162
ISBN 978-91-89504-42-4 (print)

Contents

Executive summary

The report accounts for preliminary results from the project Social Media Surveillance and Authoritarianism, funded by *Riksbankens Jubileumsfond* (The Bank of Sweden Tercentenary Foundation) 2020–2023. The project was led by Professor Göran Bolin (Södertörn University, Sweden), together with Professor Veronika Kalmus (University of Tartu, Estonia) and Professor Rita Figueiras (Universidade Católica Portuguesa, Portugal). MA Erik Björklund has contributed as Research Assistant (presently PhD student at Department of Media Studies, Stockholm University.

The aim of the project was to analyse under what conditions media users accept social media surveillance, and to what extent experiences of surveillance practices under totalitarianism, authoritarianism and liberal democracy affect such acceptance.

Taking the example of previously totalitarian Estonia, previously authoritarian Portugal, contrasted with the conditions in a long-term democracy such as Sweden, the project has:

[1] conducted a quantitative comparative survey in all three countries, establishing the attitudes towards state and social media surveillance among two different generations: one brought up under totalitarian/authoritarian conditions in Estonia/Portugal (born 1946–1953) and a younger generation without such experiences (born 1988–1995);

[2] followed up the themes of the survey in focus group and individual interviews in order to gain a deeper understanding of the ways in which media users relate to social media surveillance. Due to the pandemic, these interviews have been conducted mostly online.

The quantitative survey revealed that the older generations in Estonia and Portugal had more experiences of state surveillance in their social networks, compared to their younger counterparts and both generation groups in Sweden. Younger Swedes reported higher levels of actual and mediated experiences of state surveillance, compared to their older compatriots. The older generations in all three countries demonstrated, despite their varying socialization contexts and experiences of state surveillance, a higher trust in state institutions, a more pro-authoritarian attitude, a higher tolerance toward state surveillance, and a lower tolerance toward corporate dataveillance compared to their younger compatriots.

The qualitative interviews oftentimes illustrate some of the quantitative findings, but there are also interesting details that can be followed up in analysis. A methodological takeaway are the experiences gained from conducting focus group and individual interviews online.

Introduction: aims and objectives

In the age of social media and 'surveillance capitalism' (Zuboff 2015, cf. Gandy 1993), state surveillance and corporate 'big data' surveillance (Andrejevic & Gates 2014) through social media have converged technologically (Trottier & Lyon 2012). With the spread of smartphones, laptops and other mobile and personal media, the areas of the lifeworlds of citizens that can be subsumed monitoring practices have multiplied, including information about *who*, *when* and *where* citizens and consumers engage in communication (Andrejevic 2007, van Dijk 2014). The very same online technologies are used to both 'capture the digital consumer' (Bolin 2011) and monitor state security (Haggerty & Ericson 2000, Giroux 2015, Bolin & Jerslev 2018). Recent research suggests that the attitudes of citizens towards surveillance from social media companies are mixed, where media users, on the one hand, are sceptical, but at the same time do very little in terms of protecting themselves through e.g., privacy settings (e.g., Bergström 2015, Jansson 2012, Leckner 2018, Turow et al. 2015), the phenomenon that Barnes (2006) calls the 'privacy paradox'.

This research, however, does not explain the roots of this ambivalence. Most of it is also conducted in long-time liberal democracies, that is, in societies freed from explicit and intrusive totalitarian or authoritarian surveillance practices. The question, then, is if citizens with experiences of such surveillance practices will differ from those without. What if attitudes towards state surveillance are related to attitudes to social media surveillance? What role does the historical legacy of totalitarianism or authoritarianism play for attitudes to social media surveillance? How does trust in institutions such as government or media impact on attitudes towards social media surveillance? Based on such questions it should make sense to conduct a cross-cultural comparison of approaches to social media surveillance among different generations with different experiences of totalitarianism/authoritarianism.

The aim of the project has been to analyse under what conditions media users accept social media surveillance, and to what extent experiences of surveillance practices under totalitarianism, authoritarianism and liberal democracy affect such acceptance.

Taking the example of previously totalitarian Estonia, previously authoritarian Portugal, contrasted with the conditions in a long-term democracy such as Sweden, the project has:

[1] conducted a quantitative national survey in all three countries, establishing the attitudes towards state and social media surveillance among two different generations: one brought up under totalitarian/authoritarian conditions and a younger generation without such experiences;

[2] followed up the themes of the survey in focus group and individual interviews in order to gain a deeper understanding of the ways in which media users relate to social media surveillance. Due to the pandemic, these interviews have been conducted online rather than face-to-face.

The next chapter describes the fieldwork and the material collected.

Research design and methodological approach

The project has analysed historically formed attitudes to social media (and state) surveillance based in media user experiences in three national settings: Estonia, Sweden and Portugal. In our design, we have defined **social media surveillance** as surveillance by social media companies, that is, commercial companies whose business models build on the extraction of data from their users in order to tailor content, advertising, or other commercial offers to them, or to selling their data to third parties (well-known examples are Twitter, Facebook, and other social media companies, but also search engines, apps, recommendation systems, etc.). We have also used the term **dataveillance** for the same type of commercial surveillance (Clarke, 1988, van Dijck 2014). By **state surveillance** we refer to a broader set of categories including the monitoring of citizens by state institution for security reasons, crime prevention or population control. By **totalitarian** we refer to the type of rule where all aspects of social life are subordinated to the authority of the state, often on ideological grounds. **Authoritarian** rule mainly differs from totalitarian governance by the lack of any well-developed ideological grounding (Linz 2000; Meuschel 2000).

The main reason for choosing Estonia and Portugal is the difference between the ideologically steered totalitarian Soviet Estonia and the authoritarian Portugal, with Sweden as a contrasting liberal democracy. There are of course other countries that could represent liberal democracies, but Sweden shares with Portugal and Estonia a similar level of high institutional **trust** of government institutions, well above the mean value for European countries. Trust in governmental institutions is also increasing in all three countries, which means that the patterns of trust are similar (EU 2017: 6f). This means that possible differences cannot be attributed to this type of cultural variation on the country level (although it naturally can on the individual level). Following Masso and Männiste (2018) we expect trust in institutions (such as state institutions or media institutions) to be important for explaining attitudes towards social media and state surveillance.

Estonia, Portugal, and Sweden thus represent three distinct historical *surveillance regimes.* By surveillance regime, we mean the sum of all strategies and technologies of surveillance in each cultural setting. **Estonia** was occupied by the Soviet Union from 1939 until regaining independence in 1991. During these years, Estonia was subsumed by the *totalitarian* regime of the Soviet Union, characterized by the surveillance apparatus that was omnipotent and omnipresent in all spheres of society and 'included the regime's dreaded secret police with its vast powers of surveillance, arrest and detention' (Kasekamp, 2010: 130). The contemporary surveillance regime is, in contrast, loose and liberal, with state institutions investing heavily into earning and maintaining public trust, for instance by implementing a data tracker, through which citizens can see which organizations have used their data and request more information about those practices when needed (see Männiste, 2022). These efforts have resulted, particularly, in Estonian e-governance and digital services being widely trusted by the public (see Ehin et al., 2022).

Portugal lived under a right-wing dictatorship from 1926 up to 1974. During these years, strategies of intimidation, demobilization, and repression, headed by the political police with the help of a network of informants (civilians), promoted a culture of denunciation and values of resignation and obedience in the society (Pimentel, 2007). Fundamental rights of data privacy were anticipated by the Portuguese constitution (1976), and a set of laws on data protection preceded the GDPR (Bacelar de Gouveia, 2021). However, the expansion of the contemporary surveillance regime is fuelling public debate. COVID lockdowns opened a discussion around the conflicting values of privacy and safety; and the increasing use of CCTV, police body cams and drones by law enforcement units is questioned. Most notoriously, in 2022, the Portuguese data protection authority prohibited the telecom providers from retaining geolocation and traffic data of their clients, and access to that data without restrictions by criminal investigation authorities (CNPD, 2022).

To contrast these two past totalitarian/authoritarian surveillance regimes with a yardstick, we chose **Sweden** as a representative of long-time *liberal democracy*. As many liberal democracies, Sweden has a specific surveillance regime, with, for example, increased presence of CCTV in public places since the mid-1990s that triggered public debate (Flyghed, 2006; Priks, 2015). The law passed in 2008 to increase the ability for surveillance of all telephone and internet traffic passing over the Swedish territory was also fiercely debated (Bjereld and Oscarsson, 2009). Already before the GDPR, Sweden had a similar data protection regulation.

Methodologically the study has combined a quantitative survey with focus group interviews. It has focussed on two generational cohorts: those who were brought up and having their formative years under totalitarian and authoritarian conditions, and a younger cohort who has not experienced the same oppressive regime. Generation theory suggests that people's worldviews are formed during their so-called *formative years* of youth, roughly between the ages of 17–25 (Mannheim 1928/1952; cf. Bolin 2016; Nugin & Kalmus 2018). We thus aimed to focus our empirical data collection on two comparable age groups in each country, in order to have one group with experiences of totalitarian/authoritarian regimes, and one without such experiences. Given that media literacy differs with age (see, e.g., Kalmus 2016), we have taken a generational cohort based on Portugal, since Portugal became a democracy earlier than Estonia.

This means that the following two generational cohorts have been chosen. Since Portugal became a democracy earlier than Estonia, we had to define the older generational cohort based on Portugal.

- People born in 1946–1953, having had their formative years during the Soviet time in Estonia or the authoritarian regime in Portugal (and in liberal democracy in Sweden). This cohort would have been between 21–28 years old when Portugal left authoritarian rule.

- People born in 1988–1995, with their formative years in the post-totalitarian/authoritarian period in Estonia and Portugal (and in liberal democracy in Sweden). This cohort had not yet reached their formative years at the time of the regaining of Estonia's independence in 1991.

Quantitative data

The quantitative survey was conducted online by the Enkätfabriken market research company in September – November 2020. The respondents were recruited from the web panels of the research company and its partner organizations in all three countries, with the aim of achieving maximum representativity regarding geographical location and gender. The samples excluded immigrant populations in all 3 countries to keep the background of formative experiences more homogenous within countries (having moved to Portugal after 1974 would, for example, mean that they lack experiences of authoritarianism). However, the Estonian sample included a share of the quite large Russian-speaking minority (see Vihalemm & Kalmus 2009, for the historical and cultural background).

The planned sample size was 3,000 (500 for each age group in each country), and the actual sample size was 3,221 respondents (1,094 in Sweden, 1,083 in Estonia, and 1,044 in Portugal). In Estonia, the survey was conducted in two languages, Estonian and Russian (86% of the respondents identified themselves as ethnic Estonians, and 12% as Russians). A filtering mechanism in the beginning of the questionnaire asked in which language one preferred to answer. The questionnaire included 34 questions (with a total of 133 variable items), among them several novel and original indicators, developed by the authors to measure the key concepts of the research project. An English-language translation of the questionnaire is included in Appendix 1 (original Estonian, Russian, Portuguese and Swedish questionnaires to be provided on request to the authors).

Based on previous research, we expected to find crucial differences in digital literacy (e.g., Kalmus 2016) and imaginaries of digital media technologies (Kalmus et al. 2018) among the two generational cohorts. Media and information literacy, and attitudes towards social media are, thus, also important factors in the analysis. The **main variables** included:

- awareness of totalitarian/authoritarian state surveillance;
- awareness of contemporary social media and state surveillance;
- attitudes and concerns regarding social media and state surveillance;
- trust (general social trust, trust in institutions, trust in the media, trust in technology);
- usage of (social) media and mobile devices;
- general competencies in ICT and social media use, including knowledge about and usage of privacy settings on social media and mobile devices;
- levels of media and information literacy;
- socio-demographics.

The questionnaire was pretested in a **pilot study** in all countries in order to refine the indicators. The pilot study included at least 3–4 individuals in each country (10 in Estonia), and their responses have not been used in the final sample.

The quantitative data have been used to explore the patterns of relationships between the main groups of variables in the three-country context with an aim of developing a heuristic model explaining the formation of attitudes towards, and coping with, social media and state surveillance (see also Kalmus et al. 2022).

Focus group interviews: design, recruitment and process

We planned to collect the qualitative data through focus group interviews with six groups of media users (three from each cohort) in each of the three countries in order to gain a deeper insight into the possible relation between the experience of state surveillance and attitudes to or concerns over social media surveillance. The groups were aimed to be composed of 4–5 respondents each. The focus group interviews were made by the three project researchers in each country, and by Liina Romandi (MA in Journalism and Communication, consultant in the market research company Uuringupartner) in Estonia. They were structured in the same way, and around the same focal topics as the survey, in order to provide for comparability in the joint analysis.

The focus group interviews were not so much aimed at establishing a relation between the areas related to the quantitative variables, but rather endeavoured to explore the possible ways in which past experiences inform present attitudes. We hypothesized that education, occupation and place of residence would be important and therefore aimed to construct three types of focus groups in each generational cohort:

Group A: Higher education, different occupations
Group B: Secondary education, living in a small city or countryside, different occupations
Group C: Secondary education, different occupations

The focus groups were planned to be conducted in Spring 2021, but due to the COVID-19 pandemic they became slightly delayed, and the first ones were conducted in April and the last conducted in November 2021. The pandemic forced us to conduct the focus group interviews mostly online. We chose the videoconferencing tool Zoom, which allows conducting synchronous focus groups, is relatively easy to use, and guarantees high quality recording. In preparation for the online focus groups, we consulted with departmental colleagues who had already started doing focus groups just before the pandemic and quickly had had to move these online

(Bengtsson & Johansson 2022). We were advised to arrange for smaller groups, preferably with people who were somewhat acquainted, and to shorten the expected time for interviews to maximum one hour.

Recruitment was initially made by researchers within their extended networks. Respondents were compensated for their interviews by a gift card of 300 SEK/20 EUR in Estonia and Portugal. An email with a reminder was sent out 3–4 days before the interview with the Zoom link and the telephone number to the interviewer, and a reminder was also sent with the link on the morning of the interview. Interviews were scheduled to late afternoons/early evenings.

To recruit interview groups that were somewhat acquainted was not entirely successful. In **Sweden**, only the young group A consisted of informants that were acquainted before the interview. For the reminder of the focus groups, Enkätfabriken was hired to draw samples from their panels in the three desired groups. Despite the fact that people drawn from these panels had accepted to take part in an interview, there was a surprisingly large number of people who did not show up on the day of the interview, despite the reminders. This resulted in some groups consisting of only two people, what we have called "mini-groups" in Table 1. These group interviews were then complemented with individual interviews, recruited through network contacts. Table 1 below indicates in which socio-demographic groups we managed to conduct focus groups as planned, and in which we had to use mini-groups and/or individual interviews.

Table 1. The numbers of focus groups and individual interviews by countries and socio-demographic groups.

	Sweden		Estonia		Portugal	
	Focus group	Individual interview	Focus group	Individual interview	Focus group	Individual interview
Young A	1	0	1	0	1	0
Young B	1 mini-group	1	1	0	1	0
Young C	1	0	1	0	1	0
Old A	1	0	1	0	1	0
Old B	0	2	0	5	0	5
Old C	1 mini-group	0	2 mini-groups	0	0	3

Notes: **Group A:** higher education, different occupations; **Group B:** secondary education, living in a small city or countryside, different occupations; **Group C:** secondary education, different occupations. **Mini-group** means a group of two interviewees. **White background:** focus groups conducted as planned; **Light grey background:** focus groups conducted partly as planned; **Dark grey background:** focus groups substituted with individual interviews.

In **Estonia**, the researcher's personal network was not sufficient for recruiting all participants, and an experienced professional from a research company Uuringupartner was hired to achieve the planned sample size. The company used a recruitment questionnaire on their Facebook page, encouraged recruited participants to recruit their acquaintances, and employed personal networks to complement the sample. Due to unexpected technical problems, the group "Old C" had to be split into two "mini-groups" each consisting of two participants (the second mini-group was re-scheduled to take place after the technical problems had been solved). In the group "Old B", the potential participants were strongly reluctant to online group discussions; thus, the focus group had to be replaced with five individual interviews conducted by using the most convenient channels for the participants (Zoom – with 2 participants, Messenger – with 1 participant, and face-to-face – with 2 participants).

In **Portugal,** the researcher's personal network was sufficient for recruiting all participants according to the planned sample size. No difficulties were found with the younger cohort and with "Old A", but resistance was found among potential participants for groups "Old B" and "Old C". These people were not comfortable in participating in a group discussion with other people unknown to them. In addition, five of these potential participants did not know the videoconferencing tool Zoom and were not willing to learn how to use it when help was provided. Instead, they all suggested WhatsApp, a direct messaging app that they were familiar with, to conduct the interviews. Hence, these focus groups were substituted with eight individual interviews (Zoom — with 3 participants, and WhatsApp — 5 participants).

The focus group interviews were recorded and transcribed in their original languages. In **Sweden**, transcripts were made by company Spoken Oy, and checked and anonymised by the researcher (Bolin). In **Estonia**, the transcripts were made by the research company Uuringupartner, and checked and anonymised by the researcher (Kalmus). In **Portugal**, transcripts were made by the research company ACSV – Anna Catharina Sampaio Vale and checked and anonymised by the researcher (Figueiras).

The transcripts were machine-translated into English for reasons of comparability. We tried out several translation programmes (see Table 2) and decided to use DeepL for the best performance. The translations were then carefully hand-checked and edited by the researchers.

Table 2. Evaluation of four translation programmes (based on a test with a transcript in Estonian)

Ranking criterion	DeepL	Google Translate	Tilde	Neurotolge
Quality of translation	1	3–4	2	3–4
Privacy conditions	3	4	2	1
Convenience of use	1–2	1–2	3	4
Availability of the languages	1–2	1–2	3	4
Sum of ranking points (where, e.g., rank 1–2 = 1.5)	7	10.5	10	12.5
Preference (based on lower sums of ranks)	**1**	**3**	**2**	**4**

Challenges due to the pandemic

Online interviewing had some advantages: it was easier to recruit people irrespective of their geographical location, and to find common times for interviews, as has been identified in previous research (e.g., Wahl-Jørgensen 2021; Synnot et al. 2014). However, they also came with some severe challenges and limitations. We have already mentioned the difficulties in recruitment and the need to compose smaller groups and, preferably, groups that were somewhat acquainted beforehand. In addition, the interviews needed to be shorter compared to face-to-face interviews, and we set a time limit to maximum one hour.

The challenges can be summarized in these bullet points (for a more indepth discussion and overview, see Bolin et al. forthcoming):

- recruitment and motivation of participants;
- the composition of groups in terms of size, participants' geographical location, and degree of familiarity with one another;
- the dynamics of the group interaction;
- openness of the participants;
- the degrees of familiarity with and trust in the interviewer;
- the household status of the individual interviewee (in terms of single-person household, etc.);
- new types of privacy concerns and other ethics-related implications;
- anonymization of qualitative data.

Concerning the last two bullet points, it was found that the fact that focus groups were conducted in people's homes produced less control of the ethical situation of the researcher: we were not always aware of if there were others present in the room with the informant, which could have had an influence on how the informant responded. Moreover, especially older respondents were seldom making arrangements for protecting their privacy by, for example, blurring the image background or placing themselves in a neutral setting. Younger people were more careful in how they presented themselves on screen. We also introduced the interviews by saying that the camera could be turned off, but most respondents kept it on. From the experiences of having focus groups migrate to online mode, we drew the following three broader conclusions:

- Group size and communication dynamics need to be adjusted to the online setting, and to our experience, smaller groups of maximum five participants is beneficial for smooth turn-taking among participants.
- Participants' digital skills, familiarity with the medium, and educational and vocational background are crucial factors, and it requires flexibility in choosing interviewing tools in order to build trust in technology and in the interviewer and overcome insecurities among participants.
- There is a need for additional ethical considerations when planning and executing interviews in online space. The change to online also impacts on the analysis, and, there are also privacy implications involved when the interviews are shared between researchers.

Analysis: some descriptive research findings

The data is both quantitative and qualitative, and below we present some descriptive results regarding trust and surveillance as well as an account of the indices that were composed from the variables. We then give some examples from the interview material.

Quantitative data on trust and surveillance

Our analysis has been comparative in two respects: both between national surveillance regimes and between generations. One of the main variables of importance has been trust – individual trust in other people and in institutions. Figures 1–5 account for the data on trust.

Figure 1. Trust in other people (%).

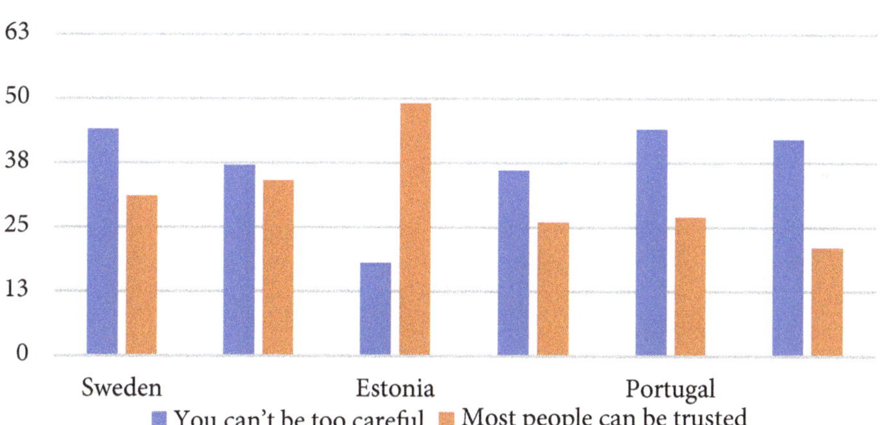

Note: Responses to the question: "Would you say that most people can be trusted, or that you can't be too careful in dealing with people?".

As seen in Figure 1, Estonia and Portugal display quite similar patterns where the older generational cohorts are more trusting of other people. In Estonia, the difference is very dramatic. To the contrary of this, in Sweden, the younger cohort has a higher trust in other people than the older cohort does, but there are still more respondents who agree with the statement that "you can't be too careful" than those who agree that "most people can be trusted". In general, Swedish respondents have a higher trust, while the Portuguese respondents are the least trusting.

Figure 2. Trust in government (%).

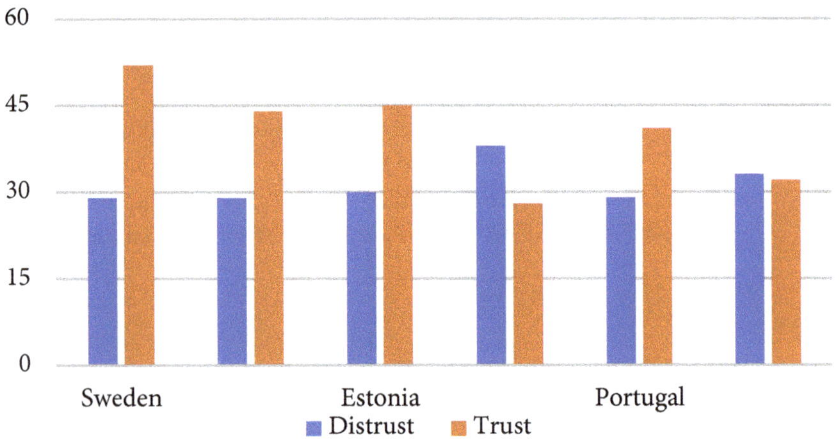

Note: The degree to which respondents agree/disagree with the statement: "To what extent do you trust the following institutions and groups? (The Government)".

Figure 2 allows concluding that trust in government is relatively high in Sweden among both cohorts. The older generational cohorts in both Estonia and Portugal have higher trust in government than the younger cohorts, who are more distrustful in relation to government (although trust and distrust levels among the younger Portuguese are almost equally high).

Figure 3. Trust in political parties (%).

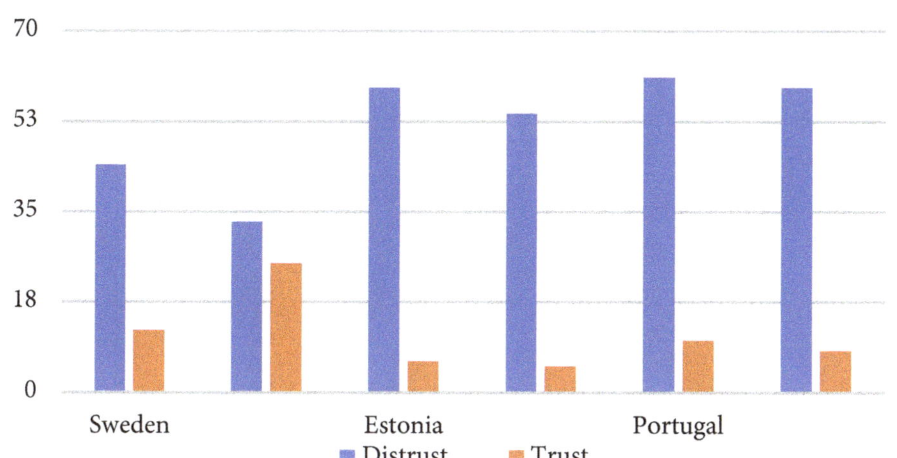

Note: The degree to which respondents agree/disagree with the statement: "To what extent do you trust the following institutions and groups? (Political parties)".

The overarching conclusion from Figure 3 is that political parties gain very low trust among all respondents. The highest trust in political parties can be found among the younger Swedes, but even in that group, trust only amounts to 25% of respondents.

Figure 4. Trust in social media (%).

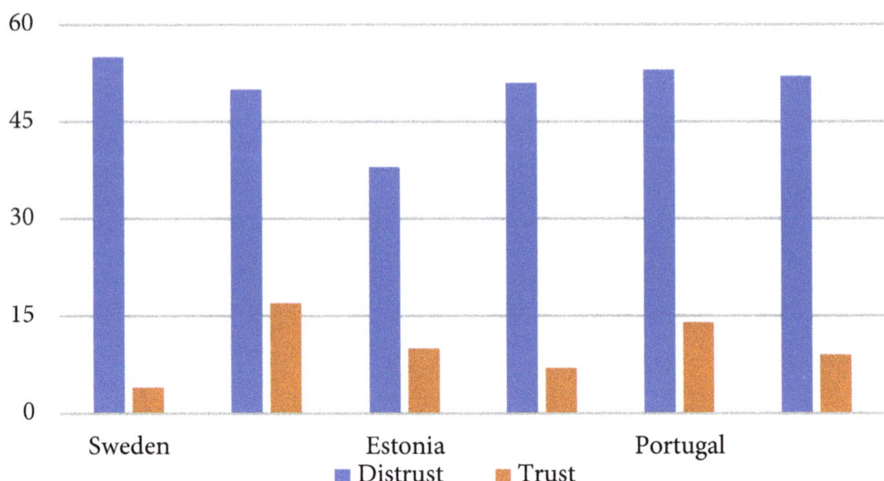

Note: The degree to which respondents agree/disagree with the statement: "To what extent do you trust the following institutions and groups? (Social media, e.g., Facebook)".

If political parties gain very little trust among the three populations, the similar can be said about trust in social media. This might not be equally surprising, since trust might be a category one does not immediately think of in relation to social media.

Figure 5. Trust in corporations handling of personal data (%).

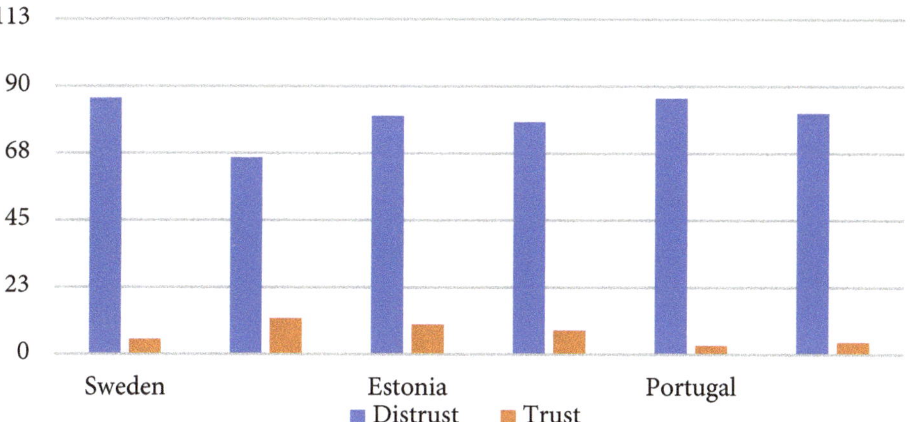

Note: The degree to which respondents agree/disagree with the statement: "I do not mind that private corporations have access to my data on social media".

Trust in corporations when it comes to handling personal data is even lower than trust in social media, which means that when one specifies the parameter of trust, people are even more skeptical.

The degrees to which respondents agree to being monitored in their online communication to prevent terrorism are somewhat surprising. Especially surprising is that Estonian young respondents are rather tolerant toward state surveillance to prevent terrorism (see Figure 6). The patterns of trust in Portugal differ from the other two countries in that trust and distrust are evenly spread among the respondents of both generation groups.

Figure 6. Surveillance acceptance in relation to terrorism (%).

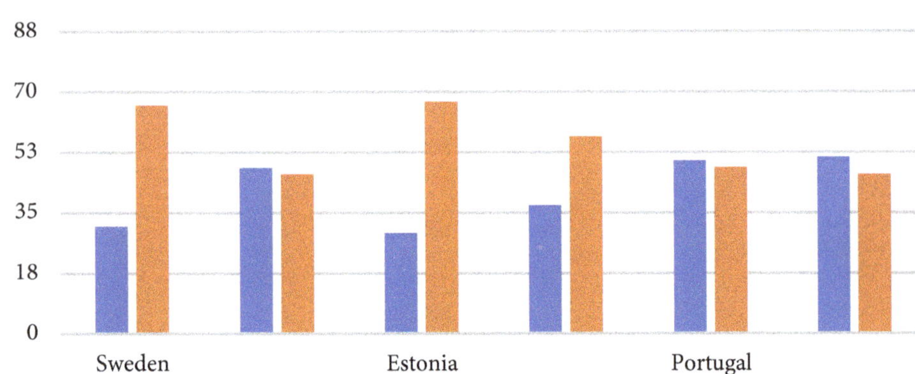

Note: The degree to which respondents agree/disagree with the statement: "The state authorities have every right to monitor their citizens' online communication to prevent terrorist attacks".

Indices

Our analysis was also further elaborated with the help of aggregated index variables, composed by summing the values of several indicators used in the survey (see Appendix 2 for the full list of the indices). The indices had good or acceptable internal consistency (see Table 3).

The main dependent index variables were:

- *Tolerance toward online state surveillance*, consisting of five indicators: I do not mind that state authorities have access to my data on social media; The state authorities have every right to monitor their citizens' online communication to prevent terrorist attacks; The state authorities have every right to monitor their citizens' online communication to prevent violent protests or riots; The state authorities have every right to monitor their citizens' online communication to prevent foreign intervention (e.g., in elections); The state authorities have every right to monitor their citizens' digitally (use drones, apps, geo-local positioning) to prevent the spread of diseases; all measured on the scale *1 – fully disagree … 4 – fully agree*;

- *Tolerance toward corporate dataveillance*, consisting of seven indicators (adapted from Ofcom, 2019): I do not mind that private corporations have access to my data on social media, measured on the scale *1 – fully disagree … 4 – fully agree*; I am happy for companies to collect and use my personal information if… I get a personalized service in return – like a weather update on my phone (based on my location); They use it to show me adverts or information that might be more relevant to me; They use it to send me relevant special offers/discounts for products/services they think I might like; They are clear about how they will use my information; I can choose to opt-out at any point, and they will stop using my data; They reassure me they will not share my information with other companies; measured on the scale *0 – doesn't apply to me; 1 – applies to me.*

Other main index variables were:

- *Experiences of state surveillance*, consisting of two indicators: Do you know anyone in [Sweden/Portugal/Estonia] who … has carried out his/her political or religious practices (reading books, listening to the radio, attending meetings) in secret to prevent negative consequences; … has been prevented from doing something (going abroad, entering a university, getting a particular job) due to the authorities' knowledge about his/her past, the family history, political views, etc.; *0 – no; 1 – no one in person, but I have heard such stories; 2 – yes*;
- *Mediated experiences of state surveillance*, consisting of two indicators: Have you seen any movies, series, or documentaries, or read any books or articles about state surveillance; Have you heard any jokes or rumours about state surveillance; *0 – no; 1 – yes, 1 or 2; 2 – yes, several*;
- *Importance of privacy*: seven indicators of aspects of privacy the respondent considers important in daily interactions –

both online and offline (adapted from Pew Research Center, 2014); *1 – not at all important … 4 – very important*;

- *Support for freedom of expression*, consisting of two indicators (based on Finkel et al., 1999): All people should have a right to express their opinions; Media (e.g., TV, newspapers, websites) should have the right to criticize politicians and the government; *1 – strongly disagree … 5 – strongly*
- *agree*;
- *Support for a strong state*, consisting of two indicators (based on Funke, 2005): Our country needs a strong government that will move us in the right direction; Instead of needing 'civil rights and freedoms' our country needs one thing only: law and order; *1 – strongly disagree … 5 – strongly agree*;
- *Trust in state institutions*: eight indicators of state institutions the respondent trusts (from the survey Me. The World. The Media, 2014; see Masso et al., 2020); *1 – not at all … 5 – completely*;
- *Trust in the media*: five indicators of media channels (including social media) the respondent trusts (from Me. The World. The Media, 2014); *1 – not at all … 5 – completely*;
- *Functional diversity of internet use*: 17 indicators of the types of websites or apps the respondent uses (based on Me. The World. The Media, 2014; updated by the authors); *1 – never … 6 – every day*;
- *Digital skills*: ten indicators of digital skills the respondent possesses (from EU Kids Online, 2017; see Smahel et al., 2020); *1 – not at all true of me … 5 – very true of me*;
- *Mobile device usage skills*: ten indicators of activities the respondent can do on a smartphone or tablet (from EU Kids Online, 2017); *0 – no; 1 – yes*.

Table 3. Descriptive statistics for dependent and independent variables by countries and age groups.

| Variable | | | Total | Sweden | | Estonia | | Portugal | |
Index	Reliability coefficient	Statistics		Younger	Older	Younger	Older	Younger	Older
Tolerance toward online state surveillance[1]	.887*	Mean	1.73	1.53	2.17	1.63	2.06	1.38	1.58
		SD	1.35	1.32	1.45	1.25	1.23	1.24	1.43
Tolerance toward corporate dataveillance[1]	.723*	Mean	1.73	1.84	1.46	1.80	1.44	2.04	1.79
		SD	1.09	1.10	1.05	1.05	1.10	1.01	1.11
Experiences of state surveillance[1]	.774**	Mean	1.09	1.10	0.48	1.13	1.73	0.79	1.35
		SD	1.36	1.34	0.90	1.35	1.54	1.15	1.42
Mediated experiences of state surveillance[1]	.705**	Mean	1.85	1.89	1.14	2.05	2.07	1.72	2.25
		SD	1.50	1.44	1.35	1.45	1.57	1.42	1.49

| Variable | | | Total | Sweden | | Estonia | | Portugal | |
Index	Reliability coefficient	Statistics		Younger	Older	Younger	Older	Younger	Older
Importance of privacy[2]	.854*	Mean	3.88	3.25	3.55	4.07	3.59	4.51	4.34
		SD	1.34	1.49	1.33	1.16	1.42	0.95	1.10
Support for freedom of expression[1]	.633**	Mean	2.69	2.15	3.32	2.53	2.47	2.62	3.05
		SD	1.30	1.56	1.03	1.21	1.13	1.30	1.18
Support for a strong state[1]	.551**	Mean	1.65	1.38	2.30	1.11	1.27	1.80	2.05
		SD	1.30	1.31	1.40	0.98	1.12	1.16	1.32
Trust in state institutions[1]	.860*	Mean	1.97	1.91	2.34	1.94	2.22	1.60	1.80
		SD	1.18	1.25	1.17	1.14	1.07	1.11	1.17
Trust in the media[1]	.757*	Mean	1.24	1.32	1.09	1.29	1.44	1.08	1.19
		SD	1.37	1.41	1.20	1.30	1.34	1.43	1.48

| Variable | | | Total | Sweden | | Estonia | | Portugal | |
Index	Reliability coefficient	Statistics		Younger	Older	Younger	Older	Younger	Older
Functional diversity of internet use[2]	.830*	Mean	3.03	3.66	2.36	3.51	2.26	3.52	2.84
		SD	1.13	0.99	0.10	0.87	0.94	0.93	1.11
Digital skills[2]	.822*	Mean	3.11	3.19	2.68	3.64	2.68	3.61	2.84
		SD	1.04	1.09	0.94	0.82	0.93	0.93	1.05
Mobile device usage skills[1]	.763*	Mean	2.44	2.58	1.85	3.17	1.25	3.41	2.36
		SD	1.46	1.41	1.35	1.13	1.16	0.98	1.44
		N	3221	553	541	556	527	525	519

Note: 1 – Scale: 0 – lacking … 4 – very high; 2 – Scale: 1 – very low … 5 – very high; * – Cronbach's α; ** – Spearman-Brown coefficient (for two-item indices). This part of the quantitative data analysis is reported and discussed in detail in Kalmus et al. (2022). In this report, we present some findings from our comparative analysis of index means

Experiences of state surveillance

The comparison of the means of the indices demonstrated that the older generations in Estonia and Portugal reported more *experiences of state surveillance* in their social networks, compared to their younger counterparts (Figure 7). The experiences of elderly Portuguese and Estonians also surpassed those of both generation groups in Sweden. Younger Swedes reported significantly higher levels of experienced state surveillance (p<.001), compared to their older compatriots, and demonstrated a significantly higher level of *mediated experiences* (through films, documentaries, books, etc.) than older Swedes (p<.001). Generational experience patterns regarding mediated state surveillance were completely different in two other countries, with the older age group in Portugal reporting significantly more experiences through films, books, jokes, or rumors than the younger generation (p<.001), while no inter-generational gap was revealed in Estonia.

Figure 7. Experiences of state surveillance by countries and generation groups (index means; 0 – lacking ... 4 – very high)

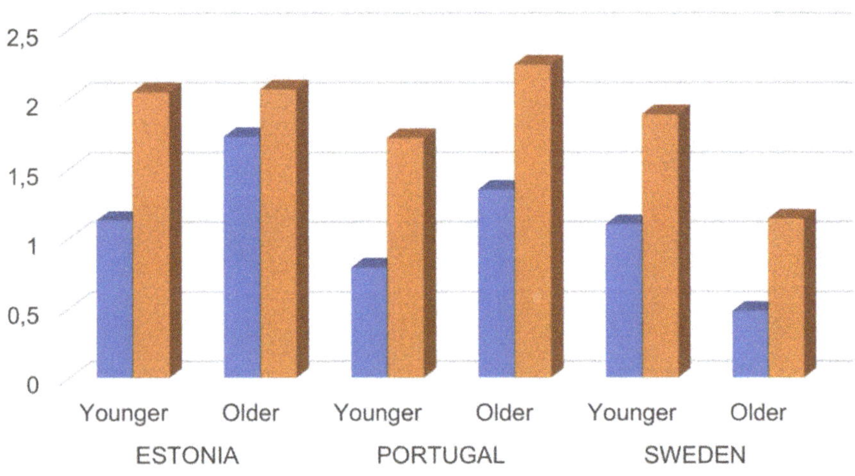

Trust, support for a strong state, importance of privacy, and tolerance of surveillance

The patterns of inter-generational differences regarding trust in state institutions, support for a strong state, tolerance toward online state surveillance, and tolerance toward corporate dataveillance were similar in all countries, with the older generation groups scoring significantly higher on all those indices except tolerance toward corporate dataveillance (see Figures 8–11).

Figure 8 shows that the older generations in all three countries have a higher *trust in state institutions* compared to the younger cohorts. The younger generation in Sweden demonstrates a higher level of *trust in the media*, compared to their older compatriots (p<.01), while the two age groups in Estonia and Portugal do not differ significantly in this respect.

Figure 8. Trust in institutions by countries and generation groups (index means; 0 – lacking ... 4 – very high)

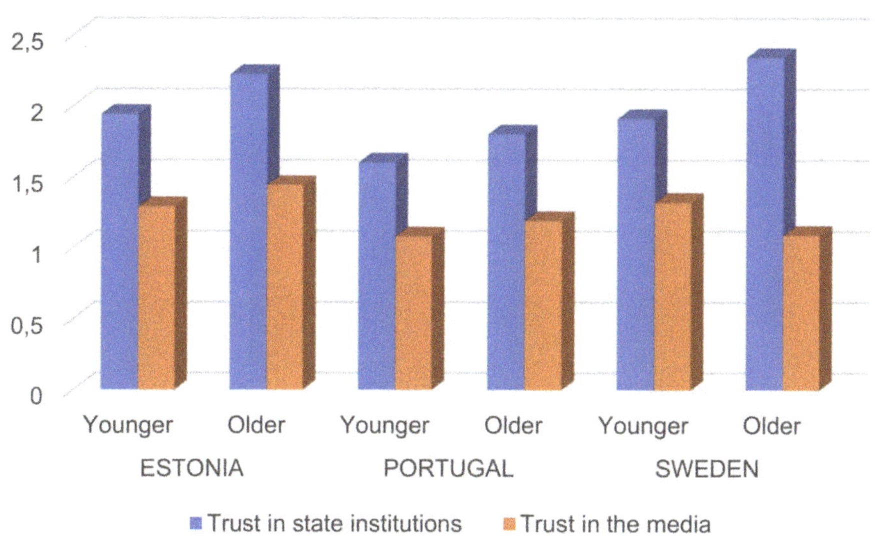

In all countries, the older generation is more *pro-authoritarian* (more in favour of a strong state) compared to their younger compatriots (Figure 9). Generational patterns regarding the *importance of privacy* are mixed, with Estonia and Portugal displaying a similar trend – privacy matters significantly more to the younger age group – while older Swedes find privacy of greater importance than the young do (Figure 9). As the younger generations differ remarkably from each other across the countries, online and offline aspects of privacy seem to be a cultural, rather than generational, phenomenon.

Figure 9. Attitudes toward authoritarian governance (a strong state) and privacy by countries and generation groups (index means; pro-authoritarian attitude: 0 – lacking ... 4 – very high; importance of privacy: 1 – very low ... 5 – very high)

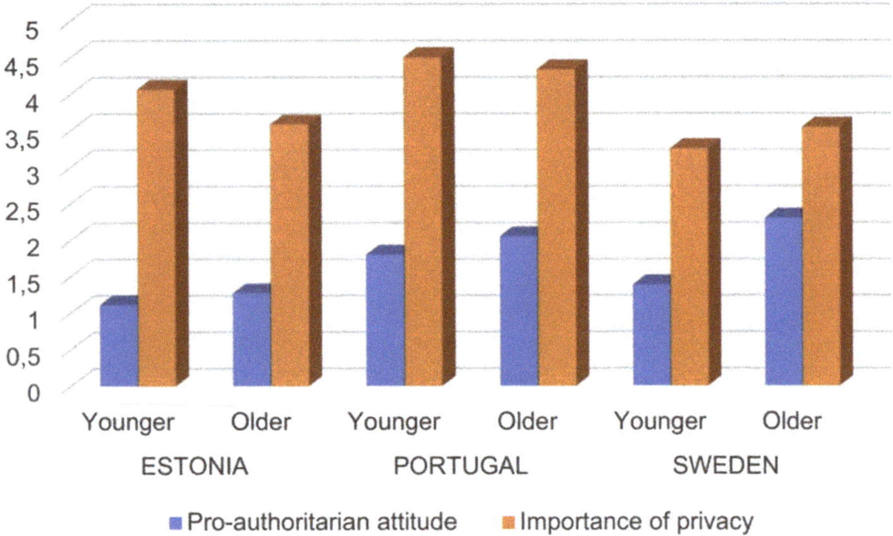

Regardless of the cultural context, the older generation groups score significantly higher on *tolerance toward online state surveillance* (Figure 10). By collating this pattern with other trends (Figures 8–9) we may summarise that older generations in all countries are more trustful, conformist, and tolerant regarding state-run matters compared to their younger compatriots. The intergenerational gap regarding *tolerance toward corporate dataveillance* is reversed in all countries (Figure 10), with younger people reporting significantly higher acceptance for companies to collect and use their personal information as a trade-off for services and benefits.

Figure 10. Tolerance toward surveillance by countries and generation groups (index means; 0 – lacking … 4 – very high)

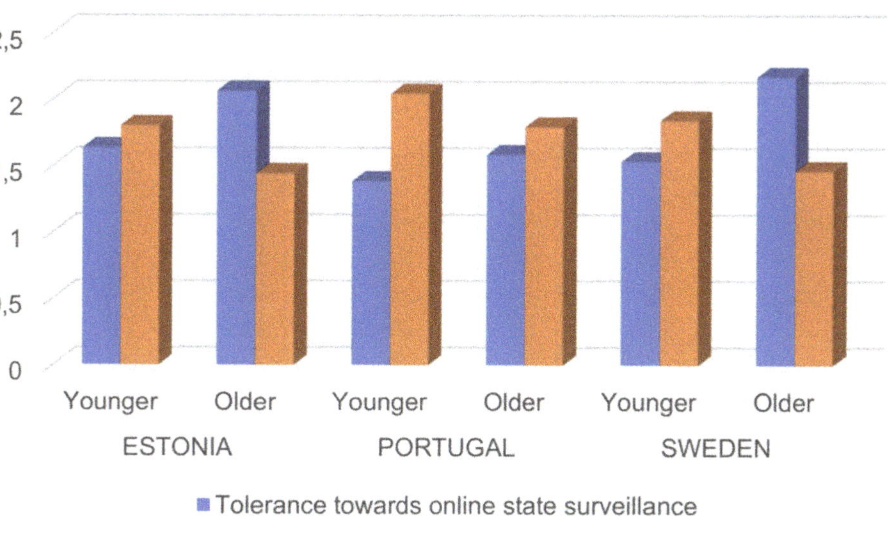

In sum, our preliminary analysis revealed cross-cultural differences in the experiences of surveillance: the older generations in Estonia and Portugal reported more experiences of state surveillance in their social networks, compared to their younger counterparts and both generation groups in Sweden. This finding was expected, considering the distinct historical contexts of the three countries. A bit surprisingly, younger Swedes reported higher levels of actual experiences of state surveillance, compared to their older compatriots. As the younger generation in Sweden also demonstrated a higher level of mediated experiences of state surveillance than their older compatriots did, they may have become more aware, observant, and critical about various instances of state surveillance also in real life.

Inter-generational differences regarding trust in state institutions, the pro-authoritarian attitude, and tolerance toward the two types of surveillance were surprisingly similar in all three countries. The older generations demonstrated, despite their varying socialization contexts and experiences of state surveillance, a higher trust in state institutions, a more pro-authoritarian attitude, and a higher tolerance toward state surveillance, and a lower tolerance toward corporate dataveillance compared to their younger compatriots.

Preliminary analysis of the interviews

Here follows a preliminary report with examples from the interview material and highlighting similarities and differences between the groups. This consists mostly of commonalities shared by several of the informants of each topic. The quotes are more illustrative of expression that are found in the material, in relation to each topic. The aim is to give a brief overview and help to pinpoint future areas of interest.

Media access and use

The most popular social media platforms among the interviewees are Facebook and Instagram. They are used by most groups regardless of age or nationality. WhatsApp is also popular, especially for communicating with people living abroad. Notably, these are all owned by Meta, showing their enormous presence in the social media landscape.

LinkedIn is a popular social media platform used for professional purposes. Among some younger groups, there is convergence of private and professional use of social media, especially among those who work in fields related to media such as advertising, graphical design, and photography. Their Instagram and Facebook accounts are used for networking and promotion of their work.

> Essentially Facebook and Instagram … and on a professional level LinkedIn, if it can be considered as a social network … but basically it is these three … Facebook, Instagram and LinkedIn… I use it a lot for professional purposes … because as what I do is reputation management and brand awareness … it makes a lot of sense to use social networks for that purpose … and that's about all I do … is … and I confess that less and less on a personal level … on purpose … is something that I force myself so to speak … to try to use less and less on a personal level … taking into consideration what I post and

what I think about these social networks. (António, Portuguese Young Group A).

Familiarity with social media

Most of the interviewed participants across all groups report that they are very familiar with social media. But there are some who totally reject the use of it. Most of them seem to be men, especially older ones.

> I think this social media thing is one of the worst things that has happened in my life. So, I don't understand the point of it all. I'm busy texting on this one. … I simply refuse. I just don't see the point of it. (Bengt, Swedish Older Group B)

Some participants in the older groups also received help from their children to set up and learn to use social media. There is even an example where the children took away their mother's accounts because they stressed her out too much during the election cycle of her son who was a politician.

> … my kids took away my Facebook… my son was … mayor … and you know what it was like before the elections … it was a bit bad … and they said things about my son that I know he's not … because my son is one of the most serious people, there is … it wasn't exactly his seriousness … they said bad things about him … and I got nervous and went to City X twice, to the hospital, almost having two strokes … and they took away my Facebook. (Manuela, Portuguese Older Group C)

Types of activities on social media (reading /posting / image management)

When discussing their activity on social media, several of the participants answer that they do not post a lot themselves and only consume other people's content. But this answer depends on what is considered posting "a lot". There seems to be a want of not being perceived as one who is *too* involved in social media and posts everything going on in their life.

> Well, I don't want to be seen as some crazy aunt who shares every… every kind of I don't know game and… and a bazillion pictures of kids, right. Of course, I have pictures of my children on Facebook, but not that we're looking at them every day from every angle, right, and there's no such, such topics. (Sille, Estonian Younger Group C)

A common response is that one does not consider one's life as especially interesting for other people, something that has been observed also in previous research (e.g. Bolin 2018). This notion seems to go in tandem with their reasoning around surveillance. Not seeing themselves as a person of interests they do not see why anyone would collect data on them or if they do why it would matter. "No one cares" and "I got nothing to hide" seem to be related in some ways.

> I don't really have any secrets, then there are things that I don't want to be spread around, but who's interested, I think, it's somehow so, I don't know, it's somehow a non-issue for me personally. Then you can think on a larger level that it's worrying when these things come out, leaks happen and lots of information becomes available about how financial transactions work globally and so it's worrying on a societal level. But for me personally, I don't think it's a major danger. (Anna, Swedish Older Group A)

Security measures

Most of the people interviewed have not changed their security or privacy settings. Neither do they read any terms of use. The respondents cite either a lack of time or ability to understand them and/or just accept whatever they entail. This could be seen as an issue of *privacy (il)literacy* or *apathy*.

> I don't think it's possible to stop it but we're probably prisoners there… Well, I think that a lot of people accept a lot of things, they have no idea what they accept, they accept, I accept and so on, but then they don't care to read seven pages… And then the advertising you get is painful, but you can't do anything about it, I think… No, I think we're generally pretty comfortable with this, so we're… I think we are. (Bengt, Swedish Older Group A)

There are outliers to this. Some of the interviewees have taken quite extensive security measures and precautions, ranging from VPN's or encrypted chat services to systems of bank accounts to prevent fraud. A difference in the measures can be seen between the age groups. The older are more concerned with interpersonal security issues like fraud and scam and the younger are trying more to protect their data from surveillance. This could be seen as a case of *analogue thinking*, where the functions of digital media are evaluated as if they were analogue (for an elaborate discussion of this, see Figueiras et al. submitted). An example of this from the interviews are these two cautious people essentially dealing with the same issue in slightly different ways:

> I belong to that little cautious type, so I put away, I have no money in my accounts if you say so, but I have put it in an account that I do not use so, but then when I pay, I have to transfer it there, therefore Swish is not a good thing. … Well, but no, I mean, you hear about, read about constantly that with the scams. And I don't want somebody hacking my code or my account and then stealing my money… I run niche banks so then they have to look around at all of them if they're going to steal all the money I have. I'm spread over seven or eight. (Lars, Swedish Older Group B)

> I've also put a block on Windows myself to see what it gets and how it can monitor or send information at all. The only thing I've left open is actually Instagram because sometimes when I post some cycling or extreme sports stuff, I've found some pretty cool people to interact with. That's like the only one that's like more public, by me. But Google and all the other stuff I've kind of shut down what and how it's tracking, because, well, if this data leaks or your information can be retrieved, it's very easy to come up with identity theft because on the black market your identity is still a currency, so well. (Marek, Estonian Younger Group C)

Lars, the older Swede, is focused on the money itself, safeguarding it by dividing it up to limit potential access to it. Marek, the younger Estonian, on the other hand, views his information as the thing of value itself, describing it as a currency on the black market. Therefore, he is trying to protect the information instead.

A third group did not really seem to understand the question or the issue at all.

> Well, I don't really know what you mean by personal data on Facebook. (Elsa, Swedish Older Group A)

Trust

There are very few who actively distrust their government; instead it is more common for the participants to compare them to authoritarian regimes such as China, North Korea or Afghanistan.

> However, I might think so if you take it a step further then, like in all this Afghanistan stuff. That they are monitoring, and that if you are against what those who are in power… That then it becomes crazy, that you can get into things because you disagree… But as it is in Sweden, and has been, I don't think it's something that I… There are certainly other countries that also have tougher rules, or therefore tough regimes. But not in Sweden, it hasn't felt that way [laughs]. (Jenny, Swedish Older Group C)

An interesting occurrence in the Swedish interviews is this distrust of other people regarding photographs of children online, especially when lightly dressed. This issue of being careful of posting photos of your children appears independently in several interviews with Swedish participants, while it is not brought up at all in the Portuguese and Estonian interviews.

> … a lot of people post very scantily clad pictures, or when their children… Even if they're small children, but when they're completely naked and stuff like that. And what's scary, I think, is that you never know where the pictures will end up. (Elsa, Swedish Younger Group B)

> Well, with the children you talk about them being careful because there is so much… well, in the sexual area. That girls are exposed to things. And that's what we talk about, that they should be careful, not post too many pictures on Instagram… And a little… Not swimsuit pictures or things like that. But that they should be a little careful. I think that's what I, or we, both me as a grandparent and the parents then, talk to… Especially with the girls in that case… They are then 13 and 15. That they should be careful. That they

don't kind of get into any sketchy stuff. (Josefin, Swedish Older Group C)

Attitudes to data mining/tracking

The most common attitude towards dataveillance (van Dijck 2014) among the interviewees is either apathy, ignorance or resignation (cf. Turow et al. 2015, Draper & Turow 2019). A common answer is that they know they should care more about it but cannot really bother to do it. Many people understand why dataveillance can be problematic and can reason about it when prompted, but at the end of the day they have resigned to online surveillance.

> No, I know that everything is being monitored, everything is being controlled. I imagine that bank accounts, things, everything goes through filters, things. But the thing is, that's modern life. (Sille, Estonian Younger Group C)

There is this circle of lack of privacy literacy, apathy, wilful ignorance and resignation. One thing feeds into the other. The incomprehensibleness of privacy terms makes people ignore them and just apathetically accept them.

> It's actually impossible to say that it does … isn't it? It's impossible to say that we read it … because it's not possible … First, they are kilometres of text … then it's a technical language that is not accessible to most of us … And besides, we're not even sure … Unless we look to see which trackers are included in each webpage … how the applications are set up … I mean … it's really hard to know all these things. (Pedro, Portuguese Younger Group A)

But there are also some very poignant observations:

> In fact, every time I start to think about the fact that all the information that I do is being stored, is being collected, it's terrifying, because I think I would hate to see the conclusions, the analyses that come out of it. So, that's really, let's face it, it's a bit of a look into people's brains. They actually know our behaviours and patterns, our psychological, whatever things we might have, right. It's scary. (Mari, Estonian Younger Group A)

Both younger and older interviewees express resignation over the commercial as well as state surveillance, to the point that they can even be cynical about it:

> Well, my phone is tracked all the time here [laughing], because we already have a business company like that. [...] ... it's clear that an eye is kept on you all the time. [laughter] For the military. And well, whatever, police databases and... (Ilmar, Estonian, Older Group B)

> Sometimes I feel that I'm really careful about what I write to friends and family. For instance, I don't feel safe to make a joke or anything on Signal. What stops me is the fear of bad reputation. It can have professional consequences. And it stays there forever, because on the internet nothing dies. (Simão, Portuguese, Younger Group C)

But there is also among some informants, a mild form of resistance to dataveillance, illustrated by this young Portuguese user:

> I stopped using social networks in a conscious and deliberate manner, because I felt that it was too addictive and I [...] didn't want to support a business model that I didn't appreciate. [...]. Now I use Facebook very rarely. I use Instagram because it gives me great pleasure, but I publish only stories that are deleted after 24 hours [...]. I rarely post photos on my feed. Only if it's related to a trip or something very specific. (André, Portuguese, younger Group A)

Experiences of state surveillance

The experiences differ quite a lot among the interviewees. In the Portuguese and Estonian groups there is a clear difference between the age groups. The older groups had more experiences, but many (especially in Portugal) did not want to talk about it, except for how hard it was to travel, especially abroad. The issue of not being allowed to travel during the authoritarian regimes is a common experience of both the Portuguese and Estonian participants. There are also some anecdotes, and stories of family members being sent to prison and such.

> I remember... because my father was a communist at the time... and he listened... secretly... to Moscow radio and other Algerian channels... I don't know where... it was all very secretly... No... no

> no no… my father never talked about it… I'm the one who already… I was the one who realized… and was realizing… there is something bad there, isn't it (laughs)… my father was very unnerved and… and didn't…talk about it… I didn't want to influence… I didn't want anything… and it was only me who knew… or my mother… I didn't… take part in the conversation… (Adélia, Portuguese Older Group B)

Some of the stories can be partly considered as "tall tales". Most notably an older Estonian man claiming to have supernatural abilities and knowing a boy with supernatural abilities who told him about secret weapons. Then he got questioned by KGB and was arguably able to influence the health of the people in the KGB department:

> And then I told them /---/, and then the director of the museum went to the KGB, he was a KGB agent, and [told the KGB]: "You see [the interviewee] was talking about something like that, about the most secret weapon in Russia", and then I was invited to go there and then they asked me: "Where did you get this information, [in a demanding voice] about our most secret weapon", I said that the boy told me what the boy told me, [laughter] it was a kind of cinema. [laughter] But after I went there, all the people in the KGB department got sick. I got a phone call saying: "For God's sake, don't come back here [laughter]. (Ilmar, Estonian Older Group B)

Maybe unsurprisingly, the Swedish groups reported almost no experiences of state surveillance.

Experiences of corporate surveillance

All of the people interviewed seem to have experienced some form of corporate surveillance. The most common example is the targeted advertisement in browsers and on social media. The accuracy of these advertisements seems to spur the notion of being listened to. A lot of people discuss the experience of feeling like their phones record when they talk about things and then give them adverts based on it. This anxiety seems to exist in all countries and be more prevalent among the younger people.

> I don't know if they track sound on the phone as well. But often when you talk about something, it comes up later in the flow… I've

kind of accepted it…Well, of course it's unpleasant. But at the same time, I feel like "damn, there's nothing I can do". What should I do? I'm kind of working with the phone. I must have it. (Alexandra, Swedish Younger Group B)

There are some positive experiences tied to targeted advertisements and corporate surveillance. For example, an older Swedish woman tells how she bought a prosecco-calendar from an ad and was really happy with it. There are also those who reason that if there must be ads, they would rather have the ones that are of interest for them.

Yes, then you get some tips on the advertising there. I bought an advent calendar with bubbles. What's it called… Prosecco calendar I have… I found that in the commercial [laughs]… it was advertising on Facebook. (Birgitta, Swedish Older Group B)

Experience of cyber crimes

In the material there are some stories about hacked Facebook pages and similar experiences, to a great extent secondary ones. Swedish interviews can be clearly distinguished by a general fear of bank fraud and similar crimes. While such experiences are present in some groups in the other countries, almost all Swedish groups discuss some form of security measures or suspicions regarding online shopping or money management. There is a general attitude of suspicion toward anything not Swedish, and the most common strategy is relying on the online payment system Klarna to act as intermediary when buying things online. Klarna seemingly has a position as a trusted Swedish institution when shopping online.

I often pay through Klarna. Then you pay in arrears, when you have received the goods, and so I hope it's safe. (Asked if she trusts Klarna.) Yes… I don't know if I'm gullible. But it has worked so far, so that… There's always a bit of that, I think… You order some trip or something… But I go through Sweden too. But sometimes it's… well, you take a credit card. But mostly safe, I think. You get a text message, a code and then you send… Because it feels a bit safer. (Josefin, Swedish Older Group C)

Fictional or narrative experiences of surveillance in film, TV, literature, etc.

The most named media production is Netflix's *Black Mirror*, followed by documentaries about Edward Snowden and Cambridge Analytica (see Cadwalladr 2018 on the event itself), although it is not always clear if they mean any specific documentary or the Hollywood retelling of the Snowden affair. Some other notable titles named are *1984*, *Handmaid's Tale* and *The Social Dilemma*.

> I'll throw one out, *Black Mirror* it may be… I think when you watched it, especially some episodes didn't feel like miles away from where we are now but kind of close like, and that's what got, and especially given how damn fast things are moving and so on, some felt more like close than others… And, I don't know, then, and they were also the scariest ones as well. (Anton, Swedish Younger Group A)

While only being named once, an example is *Searching* (2018). Actually, they did not remember the name of the film but based on the information given in the interview we can conclude that they are referencing it. *Searching* is a cyberthriller film about a father searching for his daughter who has disappeared by following her trail of social and digital media.

> I don't remember the name of the movie … but I've seen a movie … and it was recent … and this thing about social networks … and children … isn't it … that usually go to the internet and give everything and anything … and start talking to strangers and that's it … and the thing goes like that … and the father himself then goes after it and manages to save his daughter. (Camila, Portuguese Younger Group C)

While most seem to have experienced surveillance in fiction, a lot of people had a hard time naming any specific titles, needing prompts or suggestions.

> I've read a lot of things … but I don't know by name no longer … not me … I've read … I've read a lot of things … yes … but I don't remember now the … of the … (Paula, Portuguese Older Group B).

The examples from the focus group and individual interviews broadly illustrate what type of answers we received when discussing the various topics. Needless to say, they are not representative for the general population in any of the countries studied. But they indicate several things that have been observed in previous studies, about resignation, privacy, etc.

References

Andrejevic, M. (2007) *iSpy: Surveillance and Power in the Interactive Era*, Lawrence: The University Press of Kansas.

Andrejevic, M. & Gates, K. (2014) Big Data surveillance. *Surveillance & Society* 12(2): 185–96.

Arendt, H. (1951) *The Origins of Totalitarianism*. San Diego: Harcourt Brace & Co.

Bacelar de Gouveia, J. (2021) CyberLaw and CyberSecurity. *Revista Jurídica Portucalense* 29: 59–77.

Barnes, SB. (2006) A privacy paradox: social networking in the United States. *First Monday* (11)9. Available at: http://journals.uic.edu/ojs/index.php/fm/article/view/1394/1312

Bengtsson, S & Johansson, S (2022). The Meanings of Social Media Use in Everyday Life: Filling Empty Slots, Everyday Transformations, and Mood Management. *Social Media + Society*, 8(4). https://doi.org/10.1177/20563051221130292

Bergstrom A (2015) Online privacy concerns: a broad approach to understanding the concerns of different groups for different uses. *Computers in Human Behavior* 53: 419–426.

Bjereld, U. & Oscarsson, H. (2009) Folket och FRA. In: Holmberg S and Weibull L (eds) *Svensk höst*. Göteborg: SOM-institutet, pp. 293–298.

Bolin, G. (2011) *Value and the Media: Cultural Production and Consumption in Digital Markets*. Farnham: Ashgate.

Bolin, G. (2016) *Media Generations: Experience, Identity and Mediatised Social Change*. London and New York: Routledge.

Bolin G (2018) Media Use and the Extended Commodification of the Lifeworld. In: Bilić P, Primorac J and Valtýsson B (eds) *Technologies of Labour and the Politics of Contradiction*. London: Palgrave Macmillan.

Bolin G and Jerslev A (2018) Surveillance through media, by media, in media. *Northern Lights* 16(1): 3–21.

Bolin G, Kalmus V and Figueiras R (forthcoming) Conducting Online Focus Group Interviews with Two Generations: Methodological Experiences and Reflections from the Pandemic Context, *International Journal of Qualitative Methods*.

Cadwalladr C (2018) Revealed: how 50 million Facebook profiles harvested for Cambridge Analytica in major data breach. *The Guardian*, 17 March. Available at: https://www.theguardian.com/news/2018/mar/17/cambridge-analytica-facebook-influence-us-election

Clarke Roger, A. (1988) Information technology and dataveillance. *Communications of the ACM* 31(5): 498–512.

CNPD=Comissão Nacional de Proteção de Dados (2022) Available at: https://www.cnpd.pt/comunicacao-publica/noticias/cnpd-ordena-eliminacao-dos-dados-das-comunicacoes-conservados-ao-abrigo-de-norma-declarada-inconstitucional/ (accessed 13 August 2022).

Costa Pinto A and Adinolfi G (2014) Salazar's 'New State': the paradoxes of hybridization in the fascist era. In Costa Pinto A and Kallis A (eds) *Rethinking Fascism and Dictatorship in Europe*. New York: Palgrave Macmillan, pp. 154–175.

Costa Pinto, A (ed.) (2017) *Corporatism and Fascism. The Corporatist Wave in Europe*. London: Routledge.

Draper N and Turow J (2019) The corporate cultivation of digital resignation. *New Media & Society* 21(8): 1824–1839.

Ehin, P., Solvak, M., Willemson, J. & Vinkel, P. (2022) Internet voting in Estonia 2005–2019: evidence from eleven elections. *Government Information Quarterly*. Epub ahead of print 16 June 2022. DOI: 10.1016/j.giq.2022.101718.

EU (2017) *Special Eurobarometer 461: Designing Europe's Future*. European Commission.

Figueiras R (2019) The role of mediatisation in the dynamic stabilisation of surveillance capitalism. In: Jakobsson P and Stiernstedt F (eds) *Fritt från fältet – Om medier, generationer och värden*. Huddinge: Södertörn University, pp. 169–186.

Figueiras R, Bolin, G and Kalmus V (submitted) The Analogue Mindset: Conceptualising Digital Dynamics and Analogue Resilience.

Flyghed, J. (2006) Det hotande övervakningssamhället. *Framtider*, no. 4/2006. Stockholm: Institutet för framtidsstudier.

Gandy, O. (1993) *The Panoptic Sort: A Political Economy of Personal Information*, Boulder: Westview.

Giroux, H. (2015) Totalitarian paranoia in the post-Orwellian surveillance state. *Cultural Studies*, 29(2): 108–140.

Haggerty, KD. & Ericson, RV. (2000) The surveillant assemblage. *British Journal of Sociology* 51(4): 605–622.

Jansson, A. (2012) Perceptions of surveillance: reflexivity and trust in a mediatized world (the case of Sweden). *European Journal of Communication* 27(4): 410–427.

Kalmus, V. (2016) The emergence of the 'digital generation' in Estonia s transition period. In Nugin, R., Kannike, A. & Raudsepp M. (eds) *Generations in Estonia: Contemporary Perspectives on Turbulent Times*. Tartu: University of Tartu Press, 319–341.

Kalmus, V., Masso, A., Opermann, S. & Täht, K. (2018) Mobile Time as a Blessing or a Curse: Perceptions of Smartphone Use and Personal Time among Generation Groups in Estonia. *Trames: Journal of the Humanities and Social Sciences*, 22(72/67), 1, 45–62.

Kalmus, V., Bolin, G. & Figueiras, R. (2022) Who is afraid of dataveillance? Attitudes toward online surveillance in a crosscultural and generational perspective. *New Media & Society*. Ahead of print. DOI: 10.1177/ 14614448221134493

Kasekamp, A (2010) *A History of the Baltic States*. Hampshire: Palgrave McMillan.

Leckner, S. (2018) Sceptics and supporters of corporate use of behaveoural data: a study of attitudes towards informational privacy and internet surveillance in Sweden. *Northern Lights* 16(1): 113–132.

Linz, J. (2000) *Totalitarian and Authoritarian Regimes*, Boulder: Lynne Rienner.

Lyon D (2015) *Surveillance after Snowden*. Cambridge/Malden: Polity Press.

Mannheim, K. (1928/1952) The problem of generations. *Essays in the Sociology of Knowledge*. London: Routledge and Kegan Paul, pp. 276–320.

Männiste, M. (2022) Big data imaginaries of data pioneers: changed data relations and challenges to agency. PhD Thesis, University of Tartu, Estonia.

Masso, A. & Männiste, M. (2018) The role of institutional trust in Estonians' privacy concerns. *Studies in Transition States and Societies* 10(2): 22–39.

Merton, R., Fiske, M., & Kendall, P. (1956). *The focused interview*. New York: Free Press.

Meuschel, S. (2000) Theories of Totalitarianism and Modern Dictatorships: A Tentative Approach. *Thesis Eleven* 61(1): 87–98.

Nugin, R. & Kalmus, V. (2018) Social generations and societal changes. In P Vihalemm, Masso, A. & Opermann, S. (eds) *The Routledge International Handbook of European Social Transformations*. London: Routledge, 298–311.

Pimentel, IF. (2007) *A História da PIDE*. Lisboa: Temas e Debates.

Priks, M. (2015) The effects of surveillance cameras on crime: evidence from the Stockholm subway. *The Economic Journal 125*: 289–305.

Synnot, A., Hill, S., Summers, M., & Taylor, M. (2014) Comparing face-to-face and online qualitative research with people with multiple sclerosis. *Qualitative Health Research* 24(3): 431–438. https://doi.org/10.1177/1049732314523840

Trottier D (2012) *Social Media as Surveillance: Rethinking Visibility in a Converging World*. Farnham: Ashgate.

Trottier, D. and Lyon, D. (2012) Key features of social media surveillance. In: Fuchs C, Broersma K, Albrechtslund A and Sandoval M (eds) *Internet and Surveillance: The Challenges of Web 2.0 and Social Media*. London: Routledge, pp. 89–105.

Turow J., Hennessy M., and Draper N. (2015) *The Tradeoff Fallacy: How Marketers are Misrepresenting American Consumers and Opening Them up to Exploitation*. Philadelphia: Annenberg School of Communication.

van Dijck, J. (2014) Datafication, dataism and dataveillance: Big Data between scientific paradigm and ideology. *Surveillance & Society* 12(2): 197–208.

Vihalemm, T. & Kalmus, V. (2009) Cultural Differentiation of the Russian Minority. *Journal of Baltic Studies*, 40(1): 95–119.

Wahl-Jørgensen, K. (2021) The affordances of interview research on Zoom: New intimacies and active listening. *Communication, Culture & Critique*, 14(2): 373–376.

Zuboff, S. (2015) Big other: surveillance capitalism and the prospects of an information civilization. *Journal of Information Technology* 30(1): 75–89.

Appendix 1: Questionnaire in English

Dear respondent!

In today's rapidly changing society, digital media occupies a central place in people's daily lives. The digital world is made up of different social media platforms, search engines, mobile apps and web pages, and many people use some or many of these on a daily basis. In a comparative research project we are now interested in experiences of digital and online media use among the general public in Sweden, Estonia and Portugal.

The questionnaire contains general questions about your daily habits in relation to the complex and manifold media landscape. They concern both what media you have access to and use, of your attitudes to them and how they work, and more specific questions about how to manage them, for example in relation to how personal data is handled, but also what trust you put in them, as compared to other institutions and organisations in society.

The project is led by Professor Göran Bolin, Södertörn University, Sweden, Professor Veronika Kalmus, University of Tartu, Estonia, and Professor Rita Figueiras, Universidade Católica Portuguesa, Portugal. The project is funded by the Bank of Sweden Tercentenary Foundation (www.rj.se).

Your data will be treated anonymously and in accordance with the General Data Protection Directive (GDPR). The data will only be used for basic research purposes (that is, they will not be used for commercial or political purposes).

We appreciate your time and attention!

Södertörn University, Stockholm, Sweden
University of Tartu, Estonia
Universidade Católica Portuguesa, Lisbon, Portugal
The name and logo of the research company

INTRODUCTION

Do not stay too long to think about any question. We are interested in your spontaneous answers.

First, a couple of questions about yourself.

1. Were you born in Estonia/Portugal/Sweden?

> Yes.....1 → Q5
>
> No......0 → Q3

2. How old were you when you moved to Estonia/Portugal/Sweden?

> Younger than 6......1
>
> 6–15....................2
>
> 16–25....................3
>
> Older than 25.........4 → *Not sampled*
>
> Prefer not to say......99 → *Not sampled*

3. Where were you born? *(NB! Different options for the 3 countries)*

	Sweden	Estonia	Portugal
1	Other Scandinavian countries	Russia or the Russian SFSR	Brazil
2		Other parts of the (former) Soviet Union	Portuguese Overseas Provinces
3	Other countries in Europe	Other countries in Europe	Other countries in Europe
4	Other	Other	Other
99	Prefer not to say	Prefer not to say	Prefer not to say

ONLINE AND SOCIAL MEDIA USE

Now follow some questions about your online and social media use habits.

4. People can use the internet on different devices such as computers, tablets and smartphones. How often do you use the internet on these or any other devices, whether for work or personal use?

Never.........................0 → Not sampled

Only occasionally.........1

A few times a week.......2

Most days...................3

Every day..................4

Don't know..................88 → Not sampled

Prefer not to say..........99 → Not sampled

5. On a typical business day, about how much time do you spend using the internet on a computer, tablet, smartphone or other device, whether for work or personal use?

Less than an hour 1

About 1–2 hours 2

About 3–4 hours 3

About 5–6 hours 4

About 7–8 hours 5

About 9 hours or more 6

Don't know.....................88

6. How often do you use the following types of websites or apps?
PLEASE TICK ONE BOX ON EVERY LINE.

	Every day	A few times a	A few times a	Only occasiona	I used it before,	Never
1. News (portals, apps)	6	5	4	3	2	1
2. Information search (e.g. Google, Wikipedia)	6	5	4	3	2	1
3. Maps, weather (e.g. Google Maps)	6	5	4	3	2	1
4. Online banking	6	5	4	3	2	1
5. State/public services (tax office, ID, registers)	6	5	4	3	2	1
6. Health-related services or apps	6	5	4	3	2	1
7. Booking (events, public transportation)	6	5	4	3	2	1
8. Taxi service (e.g. Uber, Bolt)	6	5	4	3	2	1
9. Online shopping, food delivery	6	5	4	3	2	1

	Every day	A few times a week	A few times a month	Only occasionally,	I used it before, but	Never
10. Music (e.g. Spotify)	6	5	4	3	2	1
11. Videos (e.g. YouTube)	6	5	4	3	2	1

12. Online TV, streaming services	6	5	4	3	2	1
13. Online games	6	5	4	3	2	1
14. Communication (e.g. e-mail, Skype, Messenger, WhatsApp, Slack)	6	5	4	3	2	1
15. Social networking (e.g. Facebook, Instagram, Twitter, LinkedIn)	6	5	4	3	2	1
16. Dating	6	5	4	3	2	1
17. Genealogy (Geni, MyHeritage, Ancestry)	6	5	4	3	2	1

7. How often do you do the following things online? PLEASE TICK ONE BOX ON EVERY LINE.

	Every day	A few times a week	A few times a month	Only occasionally,	I did it before, but don' t do	Never
1. Uploading photos or pictures	6	5	4	3	2	1
2. Uploading videos	6	5	4	3	2	1
3. Downloading or sharing music, films or software (e.g. on Apple Store or Bittorrent)	6	5	4	3	2	1
4. Posting information about myself on social networks (e.g. Facebook, Twitter, Snapchat)	6	5	4	3	2	1
5. Sharing news on social networks	6	5	4	3	2	1
6. Commenting on news or articles on news portals or social networks	6	5	4	3	2	1
7. Posting or commenting on online forums (e.g. Facebook groups, ... country-specific examples)	6	5	4	3	2	1
8. Getting involved in a campaign or protest or signing a petition online	6	5	4	3	2	1

USAGE OF PRIVACY SETTINGS

8. Now follow some questions about how you relate to privacy online.

	Yes, several times	Yes, once	No, never	I don' t know/does
1. Have you ever read the terms and conditions before starting to use a new app or online environment?	3	2	1	88
2. Have you ever changed your privacy settings on any social network in order to restrict how your data is used?	3	2	1	88
3. Have you ever abstained from using a web site or app because you worry about being tracked?	3	2	1	88

9. For the websites/apps you use most frequently, have you adjusted the privacy settings?

Yes, I have……………………………………………4

Yes, but someone else helped me…………………3

I have wanted to, but don't know how to do it………2

No……………………………………………………1

I don't know……………………………………………88

10. Have you deleted anything you have previously posted from your social media accounts?

Yes, several times..................3

Yes, once or twice..................2

No, never...........................1

I do not use social media..........0

I don't know.........................88

11. Have you ever asked anyone to delete personal information about you online?

Yes, another person...1

Yes, a company/a public office...................................2

Yes, both another person and a company/
a public office 3

No...0

I don't know...88

12. How important do you find data protection and privacy issues in your life?

Very important..............4

Rather important...........3

Rather not important......2

Not at all important........1

I don't know................88

13. How well informed do you consider yourself about data protection and privacy rights?

Very well informed............................4

Rather well informed..........................3

Rather poorly informed.......................2

Very poorly informed.........................1

I don't want to be informed about it.......0

FAMILIARITY WITH ONLINE MEDIA TECHNOLOGY

14. Please indicate how true the following things are of you when thinking about how you use technologies such as the internet and smartphones. If you don't know what the question is referring to, choose the option 'I don't know'. PLEASE TICK ONE BOX ON EVERY LINE.

	Not at all true of me	Somewhat not true of	Neither true nor not true	Somewhat true of me	Very true of me	I don' t know
1. I find it easy to choose the best keywords for online searches	1	2	3	4	5	88
2. I find it easy to find a website I have visited before	1	2	3	4	5	88
3. I find it easy to decide if information online can be trusted	1	2	3	4	5	88
4. I know which information I should and shouldn't share online	1	2	3	4	5	88
5. I know how to change who I share online content with (e.g. friends, friends of friends, or everyone)	1	2	3	4	5	88
6. I know how to remove people from my contact lists	1	2	3	4	5	88
7. I know how to take part in online public debates	1	2	3	4	5	88
8. I know how to distinguish real vs. fake news	1	2	3	4	5	88

9. I know how companies and governments track people's online behaviour	1	2	3	4	5	88
10. I know how to use a programming language (e.g. Python, C, Java, etc)	1	2	3	4	5	88

15. Do you use a smartphone or tablet?

No.......0 → Q17

Yes......1 → Q16

16. Do you know how to do these things on a smartphone or tablet? PLEASE TICK ONE BOX ON EVERY LINE

	Yes	No	I don't know
1. **Connect to a Wi-Fi network**	1	0	88
2. **Have the same documents, contacts or apps on all devices that I use (e.g. smartphone, tablet, PC)**	1	0	88
3. **Update my status on the social networking site I use the most**	1	0	88
4. **Take a picture or a video with my smartphone and post it onto social media**	1	0	88
5. **Install apps on a mobile device (e.g., phone or tablet)**	1	0	88
6. **Compare similar apps to choose the one that is most reliable**	1	0	88
7. **Block pop-ups which promote apps, games or services (unrequested windows that appear during web surfing)**	1	0	88
8. **Protect a smartphone with a PIN, a screen pattern or fingerprint**	1	0	88
9. **Deactivate the function showing my geographical position (on Facebook, Google Maps, etc.)**	1	0	88
10. **Find information on how to use smartphones safely**	1	0	88

TRUST

In this section we ask to what extent you trust the media and other societal institutions and organisations.

17. Generally speaking, would you say that most people can be trusted, or that you can't be too careful in dealing with people? Please choose a score of 1 to 5, where 1 means you can't be too careful and 5 means that most people can be trusted.

You can't be too careful

1

2

3

4

5

Most people can be trusted

I don't know…………..88

Prefer not to say……..99

18. To what extent do you trust the following institutions and groups?

	Completely	To a large extent	Neither large nor small	To a small extent	Not at all	I don't know
State institutions						
1. The Estonian/Swedish/ Portuguese state	5	4	3	2	1	88
2. Government	5	4	3	2	1	88
3. The parliament	5	4	3	2	1	88
4. Police	5	4	3	2	1	88
5. The army/The Defence Forces	5	4	3	2	1	88
6. The courts	5	4	3	2	1	88
7. The Bank of Sweden/Eesti Pank/ Banco de Portugal	5	4	3	2	1	88
8. Health care	5	4	3	2	1	88
9. The European Commission	5	4	3	2	1	88
	Completely				Not at all	I don't know
Other institutions						
10. Political parties	5	4	3	2	1	88
11. The municipal authorities	5	4	3	2	1	88
12. The church	5	4	3	2	1	88

13. Universities	5	4	3	2	1	88
14. Schools	5	4	3	2	1	88
15. Commercial banks	5	4	3	2	1	88
16. Large corporations	5	4	3	2	1	88
The media						
17. The daily press	5	4	3	2	1	88
18. Public service broadcasting (TV and radio)	5	4	3	2	1	88
19. Private TV channels	5	4	3	2	1	88
20. Private radio channels	5	4	3	2	1	88
21. Social media (e.g. Facebook)	5	4	3	2	1	88

ATTITUDES ON PRIVACY AND HOW ONLINE COMPANIES HANDLE YOUR DATA

In this section we would like to know your opinion on personal integrity and privacy.

19. Please read the following statements. To what extent do you agree with them? PLEASE TICK ONE BOX ON EVERY LINE.

	Fully disagree	Partly disagree	Partly agree	Fully agree	I don' t know
1. I do not mind that state authorities have access to my data on social media.	1	2	3	4	88
2. I do not mind that private corporations have access to my data on social media.	1	2	3	4	88
3. The state authorities have every right to monitor their citizens' online communication to prevent terrorist attacks	1	2	3	4	88
4. The state authorities have every right to monitor their citizens' online communication to prevent violent protests or riots	1	2	3	4	88
5. The state authorities have every right to monitor their citizens' online communication to prevent foreign intervention (e.g. in elections)	1	2	3	4	88
6. The state authorities have every right to monitor their citizens' digitally (use drones, apps, geolocal positioning) to prevent the spread of diseases.	1	2	3	4	88

Please read the full list of statements about how people feel about online companies collecting and using their personal information. PLEASE TICK ONE BOX ON EVERY LINE.

20. I am happy for companies to collect and use my personal information if...

	Applies to me	Doesn't apply to me	I don't know
1. I get a personalised service in return – like a weather update on my phone (based on my location)	1	0	88
2. They use it to show me adverts or information that might be more relevant to me	1	0	88
3. They use it to send me relevant special offers/discounts for products/services they think I might like	1	0	88
4. They are clear about how they will use my information	1	0	88
5. I can choose to opt-out at any point, and they will stop using my data	1	0	88
6. They reassure me they will not share my information with other companies	1	0	88

21. How much control do you feel you have over the information you provide online, e.g. the ability to correct, change or delete this information?

Complete control……..3   → *Go to Q23*

Partial control…………2

No control at all………1

I don't know…………..88

22. How concerned are you about not having complete control over the information you provide online? Would you say you are…?

Very concerned…………4

Fairly concerned…………3

Not very concerned………2

Not at all concerned………1

I don't know……………88

23. Privacy means different things to different people today. In thinking about all of your daily interactions – both online and offline – please say how important each of the following are to you…

	Very important	Somewhat important	Not very important	Not at all important	Don't know/ doesn't apply	Prefer not to say
1. **Being in control of who can get information about you**	4	3	2	1	88	99
2. **Not having someone watch you or listen to you without your permission**	4	3	2	1	88	99
3. **Controlling what information is collected about you**	4	3	2	1	88	99
4. **Having individuals in social and work situations not ask you things that are highly personal**	4	3	2	1	88	99
5. **Being able to share confidential matters with someone you trust**	4	3	2	1	88	99
6. **Not being monitored at work**	4	3	2	1	88	99
7. **Being able to go around in public without always being identified**	4	3	2	1	88	99

24. Have you ever felt that any institutions, companies or people intrude on your privacy using the internet or social media? PLEASE TICK ONE BOX ON EVERY LINE.

	Constantly, very often	Quite often, repeatedly	Sometimes	Seldom	Never	Don' t know/ doesn' t apply	Prefer not to say
1. State authority institutions (the tax office, police, etc)	5	4	3	2	1	88	99
2. Local government	5	4	3	2	1	88	99
3. My employer	5	4	3	2	1	88	99
4. Business companies	5	4	3	2	1	88	99
5. The health system	5	4	3	2	1	88	99
6. The education system	5	4	3	2	1	88	99
7. Strangers	5	4	3	2	1	88	99
8. Friends, acquaintances	5	4	3	2	1	88	99
9. Family members	5	4	3	2	1	88	99

25. How much do you agree or disagree with the following statements?

	Strongly disagree	Mostly disagree	Neither disagree nor agree	Mostly agree	Strongly agree
1. All people should have a right to express their opinions.	1	2	3	4	5
2. Our country needs a strong government that will move us in the right direction.	1	2	3	4	5
3. Media (e.g. TV, newspapers, websites) should have the right to criticize politicians and the government.	1	2	3	4	5
4. Instead of needing 'civil rights and freedoms' our country needs one thing only: law and order.	1	2	3	4	5

EXPERIENCES OF STATE SURVEILLANCE

In this section we are interested to know about the past experiences of state surveillance, either your own experiences or of others, for example, older relatives. Please consider the period back until the 1930s.

26. Do you know anyone in [Sweden/Portugal/Estonia] who has carried out his/her political or religious practices (reading books, listening to the radio, attending meetings) in secret to prevent negative consequences?

Yes……………………………………………………………….2

No one in person, but I have heard such stories……1

No……………………………………………………………….0

Prefer not to say……………………………………………99

27. Do you know anyone in [Sweden/Portugal/Estonia] who has been prevented from doing something (going abroad, entering a university, getting a particular job) due to the authorities' knowledge about his/her past, the family history, political views, etc?

Yes…………………………………………………………….2

No one in person, but I have heard such stories……1

No……………………………………………………………..0

Prefer not to say……………………………………………99

28. Have you seen any movies, series or documentaries, or read any books or articles about state surveillance?

Yes, several...................2

Yes, 1 or 2.....................1

No / cannot remember......0

29. Have you heard any jokes or rumours about state surveillance?

Yes, several...................2

Yes, 1 or 2.....................1

No / cannot remember......0

SOCIO-DEMOGRAPHICS

Most of the questions have now been answered. The last questions are needed for the purpose of analysing your answers together with other respondents who resemble you in terms of gender, education or some other characteristics.

30. What is the highest level of education that you have completed?

Pre-school / I have never been to school…………………………..1

Primary (3–6 years)……………………………………………2

Basic (7–9 years)………………………………………3

Secondary (10–13 years)……………………………………..4

Applied higher education/incomplete university education……5

University degree………………………………………6

Prefer not to say………………………………………99

31. Do you work or study? Which of these descriptions <u>best</u> describes your situation?

In paid work, or entrepreneur or self-employed.................1

In education 2

In paid work and in education..3

Unemployed...4

Retired..5

Retired and in part-time / extra work 6

Other (e.g. doing housework, looking after children

or other persons)..7

Prefer not to say...99

32. What is the main field of your work? If you do not work currently, please indicate the field that best characterizes your previous work life and/or education.

Agriculture, farming, forestry, hunting industry, fishery………..1

Industry, energetics, construction…………………………………….2

Service industries, commerce, transportation………………….3

Information technology, telecommunication……………………….4

Banking, insurance, real estate……………………………………5

State services, governance, social services, health service……6

Education, science…………………………………………..7

Media, culture, entertainment, sport……………………………….8

Other……………………………………………………….9

Prefer not to say…………………………………………………….99

33. Are you a citizen of [Sweden/Portugal/Estonia]?

Yes…………………….1

No………………….2

Prefer not to say……..99

34. What is your gender?

Female....1

Male........2

Other.......3

This is the end of the questionnaire. Thank you very much for your time!

Appendix 2: The composition and standardization (shortening) of indices

A. Digital media usage and skills

i1. Functional diversity of internet use

Q6_1 – Q6_17: 6=4 p, 5=3 p, 4=2 p, 3=1 p; max = 68

is1 (short):

0–22 = 1 (very low)

23–29 = 2 (low)

30–38 = 3 (moderate)

39–45 = 4 (high)

46–68 = 5 (very high)

i2. Web-based self-expression

Q7_1 – Q7_8: 6=4 p, 5=3 p, 4=2 p, 3=1 p; max = 32

is2 (short):

0–1 = 1 (very low)

2–5 = 2 (low)

6–10 = 3 (moderate)

11–17 = 4 (high)

18–32 = 5 (very high)

i3. Digital skills

Q14_1 – Q14_10: 5 or 4 = 1 p; max = 10

is3 (short):

0–1 = 1 (very low)

2–4 = 2 (low)

5–7 = 3 (moderate)

8–9 = 4 (high)

10 = 5 (very high)

i4. Mobile device usage skills

Q16_1 – Q16_10: 1=1 p; max = 10

is4 (short):

0 = 0 (lacking)

1–6 = 1 (low)

7–8 = 2 (moderate)

9 = 3 (high)

10 = 4 (very high)

B. Trust and political attitudes

i5. Trust in state institutions

Q18_1 – Q18_8: 5=2 p, 4=1 p; max = 16

is5 (short):

0 = 0 (lacking)

1–3 = 1 (low)

4–6 = 2 (moderate)

7–10 = 3 (high)

11–16 = 4 (very high)

i6. Trust in the media

Q18_17 – Q18_21: 5=2 p, 4=1 p; max = 10

is6 (short):

0 = 0 (lacking)

1 = 1 (low)

2 = 2 (moderate)

3–4 = 3 (high)

5–10 = 4 (very high)

i7. General trust in institutions

Q18_1 – Q18_21: 5=2 p, 4=1 p; max = 42

is7 (short):

0–1 = 1 (very low)

2–5 = 2 (low)

6–12 = 3 (moderate)

13–18 = 4 (high)

19–42 = 5 (very high)

i8. Support for freedom of expression (pro-democratic attitude)

Q25_1, Q25_3: 5=2 p, 4=1 p; max = 4

0 (lacking)

1 (low)

2 (moderate)

3 (high)

4 (very high)

i9. Support for a strong state (pro-authoritarian attitude)

Q25_2, Q25_4: 5=2 p, 4=1 p; max = 4

0 (lacking)

1 (low)

2 (moderate)

3 (high)

4 (very high)

C. Privacy and surveillance: attitudes, experiences and practices

i10. Online privacy practices

Q8_1 – Q8_3: 3 or 2 = 1 p;

Q9: 4 or 3 = 1 p;

Q10: 3 or 2 =1 p;

Q11_all: 1=1 p; max = 6

is10 (short):

0 = 0 (lacking)

1–2 = 1 (low)

3–4 = 2 (moderate)

5 = 3 (high)

6 = 4 (very high)

i11. Tolerance toward online surveillance

Q19_1 – Q19_6: 4=2 p, 3=1 p; max = 12

is11 (short):

0 = 0 (lacking)

1 = 1 (low)

2–4 = 2 (moderate)

5–7 = 3 (high)

8–12 = 4 (very high)

i12. Tolerance toward corporate dataveillance

Q20_1 – Q20_6: 1=1 p; max = 6

is12 (short):

0 = 0 (lacking)

1–2 = 1 (low)

3 = 2 (moderate)

4–5 = 3 (high)

6 = 4 (very high)

i13. Importance of privacy

Q23_1 – Q23_7: 4 or 3 = 1 p; max = 7

is13 (short):

0–2 = 1 (very low)

3–4 = 2 (low)

5 = 3 (moderate)

6 = 4 (high)

7 = 5 (very high)

i14. Intrusion on privacy on the internet or social media

Q24_1 – Q24_9: 5=4 p, 4=3 p, 3=2 p, 2=1 p; max = 36

is14 (short):

0 = 0 (lacking)

1–2 = 1 (low)

3–9 = 2 (moderate)

10–17 = 3 (high)

18–36 = 4 (very high)

i15. Experiences of state surveillance

Q26 – Q27: 2=2 p, 1=1 p; max = 4

0 (lacking)

1 (low)

2 (moderate)

3 (high)

4 (very high)

i16. Mediated experiences of state surveillance

Q28 – Q29: 2=2 p, 1=1 p; max = 4

0 (lacking)

1 (low)

2 (moderate)

3 (high)

4 (very high)

i17. Tolerance toward online state surveillance

Q19_1, Q19_3 – Q19_6: 4=2 p, 3=1 p; max = 10

is17 (short):

0 = 0 (lacking)

1 = 1 (low)

2–4 = 2 (moderate)

5–6 = 3 (high)

7–10 = 4 (very high)

i18. Tolerance toward corporate dataveillance (full)

Q19_1: 4=2 p, 3=1 p; Q20_1 – Q20_6: 1=1 p; max = 8

is18 (shortened):

0 = 0 (lacking)

1–2 = 1 (low)

3–4 = 2 (moderate)

5–6 = 3 (high)

7–8 = 4 (very high)